BLESSED

FROM MISERY TO MINISTRY

JAY PARKER

ISBN: **9798218539467**

DEDICATION

I want to dedicate this book to my spiritual mom and dad in the Lord and my brothers and sisters in Christ from Gospel Tabernacle Outreach Ministries Inc.

Bishop Clarence E. Lassiter and his beautiful wife Reverand Marilyn Lassiter, poured so much into me and my family. They helped guide us into the people of God we are today. My GTOMI Family has been there for us through twenty-four years of ups and downs in family life, marriage, sickness, and financial difficulties. We are profoundly grateful for all we have learned from them and the love and support they have continued to show. So, to my overseers, spiritual parents, brothers and sisters in Christ, and my blessings from God Thank You! Without you, this would never have been possible. I am blessed to have called you my Family in the household of faith. Also, to my beautiful wife of 27 years Valeska Parker, who helped me grow as well as prayed for me (and over me) even when I drove her crazy. Thank you, My Love. You see me with the eyes of God and look beyond my faults and failures. I love and cherish you always.

Love You All.

Evangelist Jay Parker.

TABLE OF CONTENTS

ACKNOWLEDGMENTS

First and foremost, all Praise, Honor, and Glory to the one true King of kings and Lord of lords Jesus Christ. None of this is possible without my God.

To each one of my children, Quamaine, Darlisha, Jaynelle Michayla and Tehya. I love you all and I am so proud to say I am the father of 5 amazing kids.

To Valeska Parker aka My Love. I thank my Lord for the Spirit of God within you. You are my wife, my prayer warrior, my friend, and a reason from God to be a better man every day. Thirty years together, 26 years of marriage, through thick and thin I still say, "I DO." I love you Mrs. Parker and I am thankful you are always in my corner.

To My GTOMI Family, past and present, thank you from the bottom of my heart. Every one of you has played a Godly role in my life to help shape me into the man God has called me to be. I would name you all, but it would hurt my heart if I forgot one person. So, if you are reading this today and have served with me in ministry, then I am talking to you. I pray God's blessings upon all of you daily.

The Springs Church family in Florida, thank you for welcoming us all with open arms. We came here six years ago with little and knew no one. You made that step of faith easier and warmer.

I want to acknowledge every one of you who has come into my life whether you have been a lifelong friend or someone who was here one day and gone the next, you have had some role in helping me become the man I am today and for that I am grateful.

To my daughter Michayla for helping me with formatting my book. I deeply appreciate your help and encouragement

INTRODUCTION

I grew up in New York City in the late sixties and early 70's with a black father and a white mother, who I see in hindsight were not a good fit for each other. My Dad was an incredibly angry and abusive man who beat my mother often, especially after they had a night of drinking. My mother was an alcoholic who was not ready to take on the responsibility of me and my little sister, instead she chose alcohol and other men over her children. She tried to be a mother, but alcohol overtook her. At the age of seven my dad moved us to Stamford, CT for better schooling and to get us away from the life he lived in the city. He was always fighting, getting arrested, sleeping around, and causing as much trouble as humanly possible for one man to cause.

When I was 8 years old my mom finally had enough of the abuse and decided to leave. The thing was she left me and my little sister with the man from whom she was running. My father did not handle that well and became even angrier and began taking that anger out on me and my sister. For years, he became more abusive and heavily into alcohol and heroin and began to get increasingly more violent. He would beat me daily, sometimes because of my bad behavior, other times just because he needed a target to release on.

My Father is what many would call in the seventy's "a rolling stone." He had been married three separate times and had twenty other children out there in the world. Some older than me and others younger. A little after my mom left, my dad shipped me and my sister back to New York to stay with my oldest sister. Her boyfriend at the time wanted to help me get over the loss of my mom leaving us and thought it was a good idea to introduce me to my first beer, a 40oz bottle of Colt 45. Mind you I was only 8 years old. This was an introduction to the downward spiral of Alcoholism that lasted 24 years.

After living with my sister and her boyfriend for a couple of weeks my dad came back and brought us back home to one of his lady friends to take care of us as a state-appointed guardian. However, this arrangement did not go well because a month or so into living with her, the abuse started again, not just on me and my sister' but on her as well.

One summer day I was sitting in my backyard, and I heard this noise coming from down the street. People were in this little building (which we later named "the hole in the wall") singing, laughing, and having an exciting time. I decided to risk it and leave my yard (even though dad said not to) and see what the commotion was about. I walked up to the door and there was music playing and people having a wonderful time, so I decided to sit outside and watch. This little lady with a kind smile named Mother Gaskins saw me sitting there and invited me in. It was my first introduction to the House of God. I felt so much peace in this place and for a while forgot about my home life and felt loved. I left there that evening snuck back home, and I decided that I would go again someday.

I went for a couple of weeks and even gave my life over to the Lord, (even though at that age I did not understand what this meant), I just knew it was a good thing. I began going often and learned how to play the drums there and felt like I was part of a family. But my guardian found out one day and told my dad, and he beat me for going, and threatened me to never go there again. He did not want me going to church. He was into his incense and dark magic stuff, so going to church was not allowed in the house. I kept sneaking off for a couple more months only to get caught and whooped again. It was enough to cause me to stop going. After that life at home became more difficult. I ran away at 15 years old because I got tired of the abuse. My drinking habit became worse, I began to have anger issues to the point I was thrown

2

out of school because of disciplinary reasons, which made me even more violent. It was a bad cycle that I did not know how to break myself out of. By the age of twelve, I was smoking weed. Which later led to being introduced to crack cocaine by the age of seventeen by someone who claimed to be my friend. I was in and out of the foster system and jail and I was a high school dropout with a newborn baby and no real life ahead of me but drugs and gangs. At the age of 17 I had my first son. But not knowing how to be a dad and being locked up and stung out, that relationship with his mother did not go well. Years later, at the age of twenty-one I had my second son with another woman. He passed away soon after birth and that sent me into a tailspin of depression anger towards God and suicidal thoughts. I had three more daughters with her just after the loss of my son and then the relationship ended. Years later I met Valeska and had my last daughter with her. We were married a couple of years after that. After three years of marriage, my wife and child left due to my drug and alcohol addiction. I was ready to end it all and was in desperate need of a savior.

While at work one night third shift, a young lady who was in the office working late stopped to talk to me. She began telling me about Jesus and how He could change my life if I would accept Him in my heart. I told her I was not interested in any of that, so she gave me a cassette tape of David Danced by Fred Hammond and told me to listen when I got a chance. I got home that morning and put the cassette tape in, and a song called "Prodigal Son" came on and I wept so hard while listening to it. I wanted to end my life that night because I had realized that I was not in the right state mentally or spiritually, and I just wanted it to be over. I was tired of the gang banging, the drugs, the alcohol, and the anger but I did not know how to stop. My Life was a mess.

The next day when I awoke, I realized it was Mother's Day, so I called my wife (we were separated at the time). She

3

answered the phone and said, "who is this?" I said it is your husband I just called to wish you a Happy Mother's Day and see what you were doing. She said, "I am going to church why?" I said, "I would like to go with you." Her response was "Are you serious?" I said, "yes come pick me up." She came by and brought me to this church called Gospel Tabernacle Outreach Ministries Inc. It reminded me of the church I went to as a kid, there was so much love and joy in there you could feel it. They began announcing the speaker for the service and when they said his name. I looked up and thought to myself this name sounds familiar. He got up walked to the pulpit and said, "Jay, I see you out there, welcome." I focused my eyes and there was this brother who was selling and doing drugs with me a few years back standing there cleaned up, in a nice suit getting ready to preach the word of God. I had not seen this brother in a few years. I thought he was either in jail or dead. Yet here he was teaching the word of God and talking about how God brought him out of the same life I found myself in at this very moment. He talked about the love of Jesus and how he changed him, and I looked up and said, "Lord if you can do that for him, PLEASE DO IT FOR ME!" At that moment something changed. I got scared and ran out. Went home back to my drugs and alcohol but something wasn't right. A week went by, and I went back to GTOM again and this time I rededicated my life to the Lord. I stood at that altar and released everything I was battling with into the hands of God and cried my heart out to Him. I went home, threw everyone out, dumped the cocaine in the toilet, and never touched it again.

It has been 24 years since that day and my life is so different from what it once was. My anger is gone, and I have been alcohol-free for 21 years after being bound by it for 24 years, I have been drug-free for 20 years and God has restored my relationship with my wife and my children. We will be celebrating 27 years this October 2024.

God has done so much in and through my life in the last 24 years and this is just a snapshot of my past and present. I share this with you in hopes it will help you to see that there is light in a dark, broken life and his name is Jesus Christ. In this book, I will share little devotionals that I have posted over the years on Facebook and insight into what God has taught me that I have shared in messages in different arenas. I will also share some more of my story in hopes that it helps shine the light of God on your life and you see that the same God who did it for me can do it for you also.

1. HE CHANGED MY NAME

Therefore, if any man be in Christ, he is a new creature: old things are passed away; behold, all things are made new.

-2 Corinthians 5:17

All my life all I knew was violence, anger, and hatred. So much so that I had a tattoo on my right shoulder that says D.G.F, meaning "Don't Give A **** (You can guess the rest)." This was the life I lived and the attitude that was instilled into me by my dad and the circumstances that I have faced in life. But in May 2000 all this took a turn. See, it was in that month the Lord called me out of the darkness and into his marvelous light. The day I said yes to the Lord, this ugly dark cloud that kept me bound and angry in my teenage years was lifted from my life. I was, as the scripture says, "a new creature." I couldn't explain how back then but now I can, it was only the love of God. A little later in my walk with God, those same letters D.G.F that brought so much hurt and pain to myself and others were changed to "Displaying-Gods-Forgiveness." He changed my attitude and outlook on life and instilled a whole new perspective in me that I didn't have before.

And hope maketh not ashamed; because the love of God is shed abroad in our hearts by the Holy Ghost which is given unto us." -Romans 5:5

See I allowed God into my heart, and He gave me what my mom and dad didn't. He gave me the love I was searching for in others that I could only find in Him. I had a peace I never felt and a joy that the word speaks of as being unspeakable. I didn't know how to explain it, but I was different. I no longer felt the anger, the abuse, the loneliness, or abandonment. I found where I belonged. It was the same peace that I had.

6

experienced when I first walked into that little hole-in-the-wall church at 8 years old but at this moment, I am 32 years old and finally free to live.

I tried finding this peace in women, drugs, alcohol, people, money, things, rehab, and violence. But they all failed. It was while standing at the altar of God that I found what my heart was longing for, the place where I belong. God has done some amazing things in my life since that day, and you will hear about a lot of them. But I didn't write this to just tell you, my story. I wrote this so you will know God can do the same for you. Yes, YOU who is reading this right now. I don't know what it is that you may be facing at this moment, but what I do know is God can give you peace in the midst of it all. He can change your name and outlook on life if you allow Him into your heart. He wants to shed His love upon you and make you brand new in spirit, mind, and soul. He promised that he would make the old things pass away and make new things come forth when you come to Him. But you must be like the Psalmist and ask Him to:

Create in me a clean heart, O God; and renew a right spirit within me. – Psalm 51:10

"Have mercy upon me, O God, according to thy lovingkindness: according unto the multitude of thy tender mercies blot out my transgressions. Wash me thoroughly from mine iniquity, and cleanse me from my sin. For I acknowledge my transgressions: and my sin is ever before me." -Psalm 51:1-3

See once you acknowledge that you are far off from where God wants you to be, repentance and forgiveness begin. Now you must receive Christ into your heart and God will begin the newness of creation that He spoke of in **2 Corinthians 5:17.** But it only begins by receiving the Savoir.

7

Romans 10:9-10 says.
"That if thou shalt confess with thy mouth the Lord Jesus, and shalt believe in thine heart that God hath raised him from the dead, thou shalt be saved.
For with the heart, man believeth unto righteousness; and with the mouth, confession is made unto salvation."

Once this takes place, the Spirit of God is poured into your heart, and you have now come home to Him. See all of us long for that place called home. It's that safe place of comfort and protection where peace is found amid all the chaos. Jesus is that place called home. I found this out in the 2000s and he is still in that place now. Does that mean my life became easy once I came to Him? No, it didn't. But life did become easier to manage because I was no longer alone. This transformation didn't happen overnight. I mean it has been 24 years, and He is still working on me. I may not be where I should be yet, but the Lord knows I am far away from where I used to be. So today make that decision and ask Christ into your heart. This will be the beginning of a marvelous journey into God's newness in you. Because the same God who done it for me can do it for you. Yes, today with all the things the world, your family, and even you have labeled and called yourself, God will remove that label, and He will change that name.

2. GOD HEARS YOUR PRAYERS

"If my people, which are called by my name, shall humble themselves, and pray, and seek my face, and turn from their wicked ways; then will I hear from heaven, and will forgive their sin, and will heal their land."

-2 Chronicles 7:14

May of 2000, I wasn't sure if God would answer me. I was far from Him in how I lived, and I didn't think He would answer the prayers of a sinner like me. I had done so many terrible things in my life and hurt numerous people along the way. I stole, cheated, lied, injured, slept around, and caused so much chaos my entire life. But on that day, I figured I tried everything else to get rid of the hurt and pain, let me see if He would answer. So, I cried out with my whole heart "Lord if you can do that for him, please do it for me" and God answered:

"And ye shall seek me and find me when ye shall search for me with all your heart." - Jeremiah 29:13

God is there to be found if you seek Him and He hears the cries of those who call out to Him. He is never too far out of our reach and is there when we need Him.

2 Samuel 22:7 reads:
"In my distress, I called upon the LORD and cried to my God: and he did hear my voice out of his temple, and my cry did enter into his ears."

9

'Psalms 40:1-2 states:
"I waited patiently for the LORD, and he inclined unto
me and heard my cry.
He brought me up also out of a horrible pit, out of
the miry clay, and set my feet upon a rock, and
established
my goings."

It was the Mercy of God towards me that answered my prayers, and it was His love that rescued me from a lifestyle that led to death. God will hear your prayers no matter how far you think you are from Him. His mercy is from everlasting to everlasting and plenteous towards you. but you must take the first step and trust in faith that God will hear your prayer. God will never lie nor cause his name to be shamed. He said he would hear and answer. Believe that He will do as He says. Listen, you have nothing to lose. You tried everything else and none of it worked. Why not try Jesus today? The worst that can happen is you go on living the way you were living, but I don't believe that will happen. God will answer your call and help take you out of that life that is keeping you bound and miserable. The choice is yours today, choose to cry out to Him with your whole heart. He will keep his promise and answer that prayer. God never breaks His promises.

3. DENTED CAN AISLE

'I will praise thee; for I am fearfully and wonderfully made: marvelous are thy works; and that my soul knoweth right well.'
-Psalms 139:14

There are times, we walk into a supermarket, and we see the discount items in a small basket in front of the store. Many of these items are dented, crushed, have no labels, or a day or so away from expiring. The thing is these items are still good and can be used for many different purposes. Yet we walk by paying no real attention to them and continue our daily shopping routine.

But the God we serve isn't like this. Instead, He shops in the dented can aisles of the world. He looks for those who have been battered, beaten, broken, and bruised and He comes to bring hope and a purpose in life into the things the world walks by. Many of us are those dented cans and ruined items that were left behind, forgotten, past our expiration date, and seem to be no good for anything. But God has a purpose for those of us who are in that position. God doesn't make anything without a purpose for it. You are His creation and just because you have been through some tough times or are up there in age, that doesn't mean God still doesn't have a purpose for your life. You are fearfully and wonderfully made, even though at this point it may not feel like it. You are who God created you to be for such a time as this.

"But God hath chosen the foolish things of the world to confound the wise, and God hath chosen the weak things of the world to confound the things which are mighty." -1 Corinthians 1:27

Often in my life I had people walk right past me as though I never existed. Often people have told me I would go nowhere in life or accomplish anything of meaning because of how I looked or acted. I was called thug, addict, trash, worthless, and many other things that even I began to believe about myself. But God saw something different and when he called me out of the darkness and into his marvelous light, He changed my mind set about myself and showed me that I was his marvelous works. Now those same people who looked down on me and didn't think I was worth the time, call me for prayer and look to me for Godly wisdom. See God will take your messed up life and use it to show others that he is God. When my old friends see me now, they see that there is something different. And when I tell people who didn't know me back then my testimony, they can't believe I was once that person. See this is what God does when He goes looking on those highways and byways, He is looking for those who are the least to others, but everything to him.

There is a parable in the bible when Jesus talks about a banquet for a wedding that is getting ready to take place. At this banquet, the King invites all of the people of the town to come join in the festivities. But many begin to make up excuses for why they can't make it. Some blame work, others blame home duties and others have parties to attend. Well, the King gets upset and tells his servants:

"Go ye therefore into the highways, and as many as ye shall find, bid to the marriage. So those servants went out into the highways, and gathered together all as many as they found, both bad and good: and the wedding was furnished with guests. Matthew 22:9-10

See the King invited everyone to the banquet table he had set up in his kingdom and many will not answer the call because of one excuse or another. So, he went out and got those who no one thought of or even cared about, and he brought them into the banquet and dressed them in new garments and feasted with them instead of those who made excuses. God does the same with us. When we open our hearts to him, he brings us in, changes our garments, and shows us the love that many in our lives couldn't for one reason or another. God wants to take your mess and make it a message and take your trials and tests to make them a testimony. He wants to bring you to higher heights in Him and make His name known through you. So, when people see you, they say "that had to be God who did that for them, because I remember when." God has an "I remember when" story in all our lives that he wants to use. He wants to show you that you are more than what your circumstances dictate you are, and that you are an overcomer through him. You may be a dented can today, but in God's hands, you can be a gourmet meal tomorrow.

So let us stop believing that where we are now is the end of our journey. Because, every day God gives you the breath of life, He gives you another opportunity to make a name for Him. I am living proof of this very thing. God has brought me from the gutter to the pulpit and placed me in situations I could have never achieved on my own. You are Fearfully and Wonderfully made in the image and likeness of the Father, and He does not make mistakes. So today trust Him to complete the work he started in you and watch him make something special out of the dented can of your life. He is the Author and finisher of your faith, and He knows the end to the story He wrote for you. Let Him use you for his glory and watch things work out for His good in your life.

4. A PROSPEROUS SOUL WILL BRING YOU FURTHER THAN ANY AMOUNT OF MONEY CAN

'Beloved, I wish above all things that thou mayest prosper and be in health, even as thy soul prospereth.'
- 3 John 1:2

I have learned over the last 24 years of ministry that money may help pay the bills, but a "Prosperous Soul" is priceless. I have seen this scripture be misrepresented to lead to what they now call the "Prosperity Gospel." Many pastors distorted Gods word, and they teach that God wants us to have things, and that money is God's vision for us all. But I have learned over the years is God wants for His people to have a prosperous soul that is filled with His knowledge, His wisdom, and His understanding. This is what will guide you to greater heights in Jesus and take you further than you can even imagine. Feasting on the Word of God daily, praying, fasting, praise and worship, and attending times of fellowship with others will all lead to a healthy lifestyle in Christ Jesus. A prosperous soul leads to a healthy lifestyle because it puts your dependency on God and not self, man, or money, which all fail and lead to stress, anxiety, anger, and a host of other issues that can cause illness and depression, A prosperous soul can take you places you don't belong and allow you to achieve things that you never imagined in life.

"Now when they saw the boldness of Peter and John, and perceived that they were unlearned and ignorant men, they marveled; and they took knowledge of them, that they had been with Jesus." – Acts 4:13

I am a living witness to this. I have stood before Senators, Councilmen, and Congressmen. I have ministered in prisons,

pulpits, and events, I have had jobs I wasn't qualified for, and owned things that I could never own. I was a high school dropout at 17 years of age, homeless, and strung out on drugs and alcohol. I was doing any odd job I could do just to make ends meet and scraped together just enough money to buy more drugs and support my family paycheck to paycheck. But once I gave myself fully to the Lord, things changed, I changed. The same people who would've turned away from me were now hiring me. God started putting me in places and positions of authority, not because of my understanding, but because of His favor and grace. The more I began to prosper in His word the more I began to trust Him for the impossible. I even had a Peter and John moment.

In 2008 I decided to get my GED. So, I went to night school at 40 years old and I was surrounded by a bunch of younger kids and adults, and I felt a little uncomfortable and out of my element. The very first time I went to speak my speech impediment, that I had developed while growing up, decided to make an appearance. The teacher asked me to read to the class and I began stuttering right out of the gate. What took everyone else a minute to read felt like a lifetime to get out. All the other kids started snickering and laughing but I kept on trying to get the words out until I finished. This went on for a couple of weeks to where I would just begin to stutter and have a challenging time reading basic English words. So now it was time for me to take my reading test. I went to the building, sat in the hallway, and began to read my bible and began to pray. A brief time later they called my name, and I went into the study hall and began to take my test. I breezed through the test thinking nothing of it, finished up in 90min and went home.

Two days later I walked into class and the teacher stood before the classroom and began to make an announcement. She started congratulating someone in the class who passed the GED reading portion with a perfect eight hundred score.

No one in the Class history had ever scored an eight hundred. Everyone looked around including me and then she announced my name. The class was shocked, they couldn't believe that the old guy who stuttered through most of the lessons scored a perfect eight hundred on this test. One of the young guys looked over at me and asked, "How in the world did you do that?" The teacher chimed in and said, "Yes please tell us, because no one has ever taken that test and gotten a perfect score as long as I have been teaching." I looked around and said, "All I read was my Bible and then I prayed before I opened the test and asked God to guide me. The answers jumped off the page and the test took me 30 minutes to complete." The young kid looked and said, "that had to be Jesus, I am going to start reading my bible too."

God placed me in that class at that time to show His glory to those kids and even the teacher. See I did my part in learning and trusting God through the process. Then God did His part by moving on my faith and bringing His name glory. God promised to take the foolish things of this world to confound the wise. And when you prosper in your Spirit through His word, He begins to give you free access to His heavenly promises, which in turn makes other people take notice and begin to ask, how did you do that?

"Let your light so shine before men, that they may see your good works, and glorify your Father which is in heaven." – Matthew 5:16

When your soul prospers your life begins to look different to others. People who turned away from you begin to look towards you for guidance, and places that told you not to enter begin opening doors for you. Jobs you could never fill begin to promote you and see you as an asset to their company. See a prosperous soul for God shines a light that makes people take notice that something is different about you. It's God's favor that takes you places that fame, and money could never take you and it's all for the Glory of God. So, seek a prosperous soul and let everything else fall in place from that point on.

Jeremiah 29:11 says:
"For I know the thoughts that I think toward you, saith the LORD, thoughts of peace, and not of evil, to give you an expected end."

A prosperous soul will get you to the place God wants you to be. Keep learning, reading, praying, meditating, and trusting God's word. When all is said and done, your soul will prosper to the point people will begin to see the light of God within you and then they will know you have been with Jesus. He will do exceedingly and abundantly even more than you can ask or think (Ep 3:20).

5. NEW SEASONS, SAME TACTICS

"The thing that hath been, it is that which shall be, and that which is done is that which shall be done: and there is no new thing under the sun."
-Ecclesiastes 1:9

Over the years I have learned that even though we may reach new seasons in our walk with Christ. The enemy is still always up to his same old tricks. As the scripture above states, "There is nothing new under the sun", and this goes for the tactics of the enemy also. About 5 years into my walk, I began to notice a pattern that would appear either before a blessing of God took place or shortly after one occurred. Now what I mean by a blessing of God, I mean just before God would use me for His glory, bless me for His Glory, or reveal to me His Glory or when I would step out in faith to do something for the Lord, the same five issues would rear there ugly little heads.

Whenever it was my time to teach, preach, or be a blessing I would get attacked in five primary areas of my life. The enemy would attack my Health, Finances, Family, Marriage, or Job. It wouldn't always be in the same order, but it would always be those same five attacks. Before I would do something that God asked me to do my wife and I would get into a heated fellowship (for those who don't know, that is a big argument lol). My kids would begin to do something off the hook and make me question their longevity, my bank account would come up short or my check would be as if I didn't put in any hours that week, and my health would do some Gymnastic type things and start flipping out, or my job would work every nerve that week and would make me ask "do I have enough bail money?" See the enemy would use these things to try and get me off track from what God called

18

me to do. And there were times it worked successfully until I noticed the pattern.

Scripture tells us:

"The thief cometh not, but for to steal, and to kill, and to destroy: I have come that they might have life and that they might have it more abundantly."
-John 10:10

And when I began to ask myself "Why every time I am called to do something for God or after I do something my life gets flipped upside down?" and God brought this Scripture to mind. Then a lightbulb went off. Yes, the enemy does come to kill, steal, and destroy. And he is out to block my blessings or make me feel as if what I did, didn't matter. That is when I began to see the enemies' patterns and tricks. You see, satan does not want you to share God's word, lay hands on the sick or do anything God has called you to do. So, he attacks to stop you or attacks to make you feel as if your work was in vain. He sees the blessings headed your way and if he can get you acting foolish on your family, friends, co-workers, bill collector, your spouse, or your boss, then he can use that to make you feel unworthy of the calling of God on your life. You have to understand that he uses these weapons to make you back down, ball up and feel useless and unworthy to do God's will. But we must always remember.

"No weapon that is formed against thee shall prosper, and every tongue that shall rise against thee in judgment thou shalt condemn. This is the heritage of the servants of the LORD, and their righteousness is of me, saith the LORD." -Isaiah 54:17.

This means those weapons the enemy is throwing only work if we allow them to. And every tongue that rises in judgment against you by the enemy that tries to cause you to feel like you are not enough, is condemned by God. So, the enemy can try, but once you know the tricks you can begin to block them and resist the temptations of stepping out of the will of God.

Also, we must recognize the time and situation when the attacks occur. The scriptures tell us in **Matthew 4:2-3** that while Jesus was fasting for 40 days and nights and he was hungry the devil came to tempt Him. It is in the weak moments, the moments of being tired, hungry, fed up, or ill that the enemy will come to throw you off course from God's will.

He comes with the same five tricks at the same opportune time to get you to either deny God, not trust God, or turn from God. In these moments we are to do as Jesus did in each scenario and use the word against him. In **Matthew 4:4-11** every time satan tries to produce a lie Jesus says it is written. Then in Verse 10, He told satan to get behind Him, meaning His focus is on God, not satan. The word tells us in **James 4:7 that if you submit yourself to God and resist the devil then he shall flee.** What does that mean? No matter what, do as God has called you to do. No matter the trial or test, trust God to give you all you need to succeed in your calling. The enemy is going to form the weapon but trust God to hold up a shield of protection on your behalf to keep it from succeeding. Once you see when and where the attacks come and which weapon the enemy will use to bring it, you can then begin to do as God said and stand and see the Salvation of the Lord. You have been set free and you are Victorious in Christ. It's time to recognize the attacks. Know who the enemy is and learn how through God to defeat Him. You may lose a battle here or there because none of us are perfect. But what you can rest assured is that through Christ and His sacrifice, we have already won the war.

6. IT IS OK NOT TO BE OK. BUT IT IS NOT OK, NOT TO BE OK ALONE

And the LORD God said, It is not good that the man should be alone; I will make him an help meet for him.
-Genesis 2:18

This Chapter here is dedicated to My Brother in Christ and friend for over 30 years. Elder Leroy Hie.

While drafting this book I woke up to some very devastating news that my brother in Christ Elder/Deacon Leroy Hie had gone home to be with the Lord. So, after a few months passed, I reached out and asked his beautiful wife, sister Norma, if I could dedicate a chapter in my book about his life and the circumstances around his death. She agreed and it has taken me months to even sit behind my computer to write this chapter, but here it is. Deacon Lee was known to many in Providence RI, New Jersey, and Philly as Lee Lee Hie. He was loud, brash, funny, and one of the most giving people you would ever meet. Lee and I used to run the Streets in Providence, Rhode Island through different circles of people. We would run into each other and always start a cracking session between ourselves. We sold drugs on the same blocks, ran in the same clubs, and even got high together. Lee was known for His cars and his loud boisterous laugh but most of all for always being a wise guy. He and I couldn't be around each other long because he and I in many ways were a lot alike and of course when you have two wise guys together that would often cause a disturbance. Especially if alcohol was present and trust me it was. But overall, he was Lee Lee, someone if he were your friend he would give you the world and if he weren't then move out his way.

I told this story at the beginning of the book about a brother who was on the pulpit preaching on the day I gave my life to Christ, and I asked God if he could do it for him, please do it for me. Well, that brother was my brother Lee Lee. As I said Lee and I ran in the same spots, and I thought Lee was either dead or in jail because I hadn't seen this brother in a minute. What I didn't know was His mom's and many other people's prayers were being answered because Lee Lee was now Deacon Lee and had been serving God for a few years. So that day I walked into the Church where he was ministering the word that morning. For the next 18 years, He and I ministered to many in the same houses we once sold and smoked in. The same neighborhoods, we caused so much ruckus_in,- we were now doing outreaches and sharing the love of God. God used Deacon Lee to be a big part of my walk with him, so when I got that news that late October morning I was devastated. It felt like a big part of my life was just snatched away and the wise_cracking brother with the boisterous laugh was no longer with us.

As the days followed, I started to get more information on how my brother passed and the days leading up to his death. See the police believe that Lee had taken his own life on a highway in New Jersey while sitting on the side of the road. Lee had been going through in his personal life and the man who helped everyone else in need felt alone with no one to reach out to. He had just been through the death of his daughter and family issues with it. Then he lost his confidant in his favorite uncle, someone he would confide in and get direction from when he felt down or was struggling. No one knew what he was facing, nor the pain he felt because whenever you would see Lee, he had a smile on his face and was always worried about others more than himself at times. I had spoken to Lee via text a few days before he had taken his life and never knew my brother was struggling to this extent. I believe this happens to many leaders in ministry because we are looked upon to be strong and have all the answers and we should never show weakness when we have God in our lives, but this is far from the truth. A lot of us still struggle with the same life issues that non-believers struggle with and we need to reach out when times get tough because God never meant for us to go through this life alone.

In **Exodus 17,** Moses had the help of his brothers Aaron and Hur who held up his arms every time the Israelites began to lose the battle. In **Mark 6:7** and **Luke 10:1,** we see that Jesus sent two of His disciples out together because two in Christ are more powerful than one. God never meant for man or woman to walk this walk alone. When we isolate ourselves from others, we allow the enemy to target our thoughts and have us believe we are in this alone.

"Not forsaking the assembling of ourselves together, as the manner of some is; but exhorting one another: and so much the more, as ye see the day approaching."
-Hebrews 10:25

In this day and age of Covid-19, one of the weapons of the enemy was isolation. He caused us to be shut in with our thoughts and feelings without anyone from outside being there to help deal with issues that would arise. For some, it was great because it caused us to get closer to God and allow Him to speak to us and show us what his will for our lives are. For others, it was just the opposite, which led to high suicide rates, alcoholism, a rise in drug addictions and so many other social issues, some yet to be known. The one place people felt they could go was the church, but many were shut down and closed up. Yet places like drug dens and liquor stores stayed open and flourished. When the churches finally opened their doors many of those who attended didn't come back because they found other devices to occupy where God once did in their hearts. The actions of closing the doors to the church and causing people to be shut in began a snowball effect of loneliness and the feeling of abandonment.

Those who had people to turn to no longer felt they were there anymore. People began to only focus on themselves and not the needs of others and this caused what I like to call the Lone Ranger Syndrome. It began to make people believe they were alone and that they did not need others. Next, we started pulling away from the house of God and its people, because we felt as if they didn't care about them anyway. Then we find ourselves anxious, depressed, and even suicidal. There used to be a time in church if a brother or a sister didn't see you in service once or twice in a row, you had half a dozen phone calls and just as many visits.

I cannot remember how many homes Deacon Lee and I visited because people were AWOL and Bishop sent us to bring them back. This is what we are supposed to do as a people of God. We are our brothers and sisters' keepers and when we see someone going through or not attending like they used to, we are to do as **2 Timothy 4:11** says, and that is **"Go Get Mark Because He is Very Useful To The Ministry."** See, Mark, and Paul had a bit of a falling out back in **Acts 13:13.** This is where Mark walked away from the Ministry but even after this fallout Paul still knew that he needed Mark in the Ministry. Many of us need to go get Mark (whoever your Mark may be) and bring him or her back into the house of God. Now while reading this God laid someone on your heart. Someone you have not seen in a minute, Go get Mark. The enemy is out there having a field day with this person and God wants them back in the fold. We are not alone and as the song goes "You are important to me, and I need You to survive."

Now to those who are alone, this doesn't let you off the hook either. **James 5:14** says.

"Is any sick among you? let him call for the elders of the church; and let them pray over him, anointing him with oil in the name of the Lord."

You have a part to play in this also. Pastors, Deacons, Elders, and people in Christ will not know something is going on with you unless you let them in and tell them. We put on the church face and use the church speak "Oh I am blessed", "I am living for the Lord", "Blessed and highly favored" and a few other phrases, knowing there is a storm brewing in our hearts and minds and the devil is having a field day. We need to share our faults as stated in **James 5:16** and call upon the Elders to pray. It says YOU call on them, not wait at home having a pity party letting the devil beat you up because of pride or past hurts. You are doing exactly what he is hoping for, living in a Lone Ranger syndrome. God has placed people around you with the same testimony you are facing right now. Unless you open up and let others in, you will continue to spiral out of control right into the enemies' hands. I know what you are thinking, "Well I let people in before and they hurt me or gossiped about me." The best way I can explain it is like this is, you have been disturbed at Walmart before by customers and employees, yet it does not stop you from going to Walmart. The same goes for church. Don't lump everyone into the same group as those who have hurt you in Church. Let God lead you to that person He wants to use to help you break through. I didn't know what was going on in my brother's life because he didn't let me in. If he had, I believe I could have helped him through it. You must let people in to get the help you need. Unless you open up, you will always feel alone, and now the enemy has done exactly what he set forth to do. Don't let him win, let someone in and get the help you need.

My brother left this world with such a profound impact on people's lives, that he is still loved, missed, and talked about to this day. Many have come to Christ because of the love of Christ that was shown through him. His impact for the kingdom of God will truly be missed by many. Elder Lee, my brother, I love and miss you, my friend of 30 years. Knowing each other for so long and serving together for over 20 years in ministry, all gone in a blink of an eye. I will see you again my friend. Rest in Paradise my brother.

People check on your friends, family and neighbors and let them know they are not alone. The enemy is having a field day with people around you, and it is time to do as God said and "Go get your Mark."

7. YOU CAN'T BRING YOUR OLD WAYS INTO YOUR NEW BEGINNINGS. LEAVE THE PAST BEHIND

"Get up, sanctify the people, and say, 'Sanctify yourselves for tomorrow, because thus says the LORD God of Israel: "There is an accursed thing in your midst, O Israel; you cannot stand before your enemies until you take away the accursed thing from among you."
-Joshua 7:13

Shortly after giving my life to Christ, I began to see things differently. The people I hung out with just seemed different, the things I used to do, I no longer had the desire to do anymore and my attitude toward life began to shift. There was a scripture that stuck out to me that summed it up which says:

"When I was a child, I spoke as a child, I understood as a child, I thought as a child; but when I became a man, I put away childish things." -1 Corinthians 13:11.

I no longer wanted to do the things I did when I was living childishly for the world. I had a new mindset and a whole new outlook on life. I couldn't bring my past baggage to my new destination. I had to do what Joshua was telling the Israelites to do in **Joshua 7:13**, sanctify myself. Leave the stinking thinking, bad attitudes, and troublesome ways behind. Joshua was telling the Israelites that the same old ways of thinking and acting in the wilderness were not going to fly in the land of milk and honey. For them to get over the Jordan River they had to leave the wilderness lifestyle behind.

See I had to give over my vices and all the things that held me in the dark to God so He could do as His word said and "bring me into the Marvelous Light." -**1 Peter 2:9**.

God has a plan for us all, a purpose He wants to fulfill in each one of our lives. But too many of us never make it to those plans because we are still behaving as we did in the world. Holding on to past hurts, pains, struggles, failures, regrets, and unfulfilled dreams will cause us to stay stuck in the wilderness of life. Many never make it out of the hood because of a hood mentality. I could have used every excuse to stay where I was at in life. My dad was abusive, both my parents were addicts to either drugs or alcohol. My mom left when I was only 8 years old, I was a school dropout, ex-convict with no future, strung out on drugs and alcohol like my parents. I was a typical hood rat by every definition. But God took away those excuses when He said I was a new creation. So, I had to leave those excuses in the wilderness and move into what God had called me to be.

You know one of the biggest reasons why most sports stars find themselves broke at the end of their careers is because no one ever helped them change their mindset about life. One of the greatest sayings in the world is "You can take a man out of the hood but can't take the hood out of a man." The reason for this is because of the hood mindset. They believe they don't belong here, they don't deserve it, or they think it won't last so they squander it. But if you help them change that mindset about themselves then they learn to live outside of the hood or slave mindset. The way to do this is to let go of the things that kept you in the wilderness in the first place. The company you keep, the unforgiveness you carry, the hurt and pain you bear, the disappointments and failures you hold onto. Let them go! God has an over-the-river Jordan experience for you, but you must sanctify yourself and let all your idols go.

What are Idols? They are anything that has more control over you than God. Any aspect of your life that you have not let God take over is considered an idol because it is off-limits to God. Joshua told the Israelites that they had to leave those idols behind to move forward to their blessings.

I couldn't live like I live now, still acting like I did 23 years ago. I had to grow up, let go, and let God be God in every aspect of my life. Now I am living the blessed of life. I began seeing the true blessing of God through a new vision and a clear mind. When I gave everything over to God that kept me bound and asked Him to take it away. He took my anger and gave me joy, He took my worry and gave me peace, He took my hurt and replaced it with healing and he took my hate and replaced it with Love. Listen God isn't asking you to give up anything that he doesn't have a better item to replace it with.

God told the Israelites that he was replacing their wilderness with a land of milk and honey and replacing slavery with freedom. But before He did so, God told them to leave their Idols behind because He didn't want them to carry their old ways into their new destination. I know so many who have moved from state to state trying to find a better life for themselves, not realizing that they were trying to run from themselves. Their best life was just before them right where they were, but they did not want to deal with their issues head on that was stopping them from living their best life. But they rather change locations believing this would change their mindset. It may have helped for a moment, but only until the newness of the move wore off. After a while, the wilderness mindset kicks back in, and they find themselves miserable again.

Joshua told them "You are not coming out of here the same way you came in." Something has to change, and it starts with giving those thoughts and issues over to God. Cleanse yourself of all those things that have kept you bound. Time to pray and seek God with your whole heart and ask Him to search it and show you anything that is unclean in it. Then ask Him to please take it away. The result will be that you are a new creature in Christ Jesus and old things have passed away.

I wanted to live a blessed life in the newness of joy, and I need God to help me get to that place. When you make that request to God, be ready to have him reveal to you all that is holding you back. Then do as Joshua said and sanctify thy self and let it go. It may be people, things in your past, unforgiveness of self or others, whatever God reveals, let it go. God has a blessing for you on the other side of your obedience. It's time to come out of the wilderness and walk in the newness of life in Christ.

8. IT'S BECAUSE OF HIS MERCY

"It is of the Lord's mercies that we are not consumed Because His compassion fails not. They are new every morning: Great is thy Faithfulness."
-Lamentations 3:22-23

Even though I had given my life to Christ at the age of 8, I never really understood that it was God's grace and mercy that continued to keep me amid all of my mess-ups, flaws and failures. So many times, in life I should have been taken out for the things I had done. But it is because of God's mercy I am drafting this book and here to tell the stories today. Every day we do things in our lives that in time past before Christ resurrection, we would have been snuffed out and put to death by stoning, hanging, or just a word from God. But God's mercy and grace has been given to each of us even when we deserved just the opposite. Because of the love he has for us and the sacrifice of His son Jesus Christ on our behalf, we are blessed with new mercies every morning. Every person I hurt, every time I stole, every person I harmed, and the lives I have destroyed, should have been enough for God to say, "I am done with Jay." But he didn't because of His compassion and mercy towards me. I separated myself from God through drugs, alcohol, sex, and anger, yet God never separated Himself from me.

I remember a day when I ripped off the biggest crack dealer in Waterbury, Connecticut for something like 22 bottles of crack cocaine. (It was just after my father had died from a car accident and I was in a bad place). I stole these vials of drugs and went on to sell half and smoke half. Within that day the guy who owned them sent his guys to find me and bring me back to his house. When I got there, he had about 10 to 12

31

guys standing around and a couple of them drew their guns on me as soon as I walked through the door. I figured at this point my life was supposed to end for me on this day. They had guns to my head, one gun under the table pointed at my crotch, and even hit me in the side of the face with the butt of one of the pistols. But when this happened the dealer stopped his guys and said I don't know why, but I am going to give you a chance to make this up. He called his boys off and allowed me to walk out the door without putting a slug in me. As I left and walked across the parking lot of the projects, I was expecting to hear gunshots ring out because there was no way he was letting me walk. I made it to the end of the block and took off home wondering how I was still alive. As I look back and remember this time, I cannot help but to know it was God's mercy that allowed me to walk out of that house that day.

Every fight I had been in, every drug I have taken, every sip of alcohol I had drunk, every woman I had slept with, everything I had done in my life that should have or could have brought death revealed God's grace and mercy towards me. Many of us should be dead and gone but God has bestowed His mercy upon you and given you that which you did not deserve or earn. Because of Jesus Christ, we have as the Scripture says in **Ephesians 2:4-5**:

"But God who is rich in mercy, for His great love wherewith He loved us, even when we were dead in sins, He hath quickens us together with Christ Jesus, (By Grace we are saved.)

God who is rich in Mercy has given us opportunity after opportunity, even though we didn't deserve it. The scripture says, **"It is of the Lord's mercy that we are not consumed**." It is because of His mercy that we wake up to another day. It is because of His mercies that we see the end of every day.

Just think of what you have said and or done just today, this week, or this month. Now ask yourself if you were God would you have extended that same mercy? Yet every day God has shown His love and His faithfulness towards us by granting us His grace and giving us another opportunity to get right with Him. For 24 years I ran from Him, 24 years I have done things to cause my separation from Him, 24 years there wasn't a day or time that my life shouldn't have been snuffed out by God. Yet here I am, at 55 years of age sharing my testimony about the goodness of God and His mercy that seen me through. If you are reading this today, please understand and realize that scripture says mercy and grace have been extended to you.

God has not allowed you to come this far to leave you. He desires a deeper relationship with you and because of His love towards you, He is giving you a chance to have just that. He has a purpose and a plan for you and your life and because of this, He has extended His grace to you so that He may see it through. I think of **Revelations 12:11** which says,

"They Overcame Him By The Blood Of The Lamb, And By The Word Of Their Testimony."

It is our testimony that we have overcome because of the Blood of Jesus. For if it had not been for the Lord on our side, we would and should be dead and gone. Thank You Jesus for extended mercies to you and me. Amen.

9. WON'T HE DO IT

"But God hath chosen the foolish things of the world to confound the wise, And God hath chosen the weak things of the world to confound the mighty things."
-1 Corinthians 1:27

I dropped out of high school at the age of 17, in order to take care of my son. I was in the 11th grade and already hooked on drugs and alcohol, filled with anger, and locked up a few times, no hope of a future for him or myself. At this time, I was homeless, eating thrown-away donuts and bagels out of the Dunkin Donuts dumpsters. Sleeping in abandoned cars and the basement of the projects trying to survive and still trying to attend school. I was getting into fights daily because of the way I dressed or smelled. I had teachers telling me I wouldn't amount to anything and asked what I was even doing there. My dad had tried to take me out so I couldn't go home, and the system said I was too old to even care about. Just after my son was born, I tried to do something with my life, so I enrolled in Job Corps and got my degree in cooking. I graduated Job Corps and went back home with some hope for the future and then I got the news my dad was killed in a car accident. He wrapped his car around a tree on his way home from the city. Here I am 18 years old still strung out on drugs and alcohol and now having to try and raise my 16-year-old sister and try and be a father to my newborn old son.

I spiraled out of control quickly. No hope, no prospects for work, and no clue how to be the man I needed to be for my sister or my son. So, I reached out to find my mom in hopes she would be willing to help me and found out quickly that this was not a good idea. Within the first few months of finding her, I was locked up for assault with a deadly weapon, and attempted murder charges because I almost killed the man she was dating at the time because he had pulled out a knife on me.

After a few months in jail, I was released and given the choice to go back to Job Corp or to serve more time. I took the chance and went back to Job Corp and while I was there, I received a phone call that my mom had shot my baby sister over an argument about toilet paper. I became angry and lashed out and ended up getting in trouble in Job Corp which got me kicked out before I could finish my GED course. I was Cat 2 (dismissed) out of there, meaning I finished my Building Maintenance course and received my degree, but I couldn't receive my full financial benefits or go back for graduation. This was a big blow to me because I was really trying hard to succeed. But the more I tried the more I failed.

I moved to Rhode Island with the mother of my daughters and tried to live right, but no matter what I did the drugs, alcohol, and anger kept coming back. I ended up in and out of jail a couple more times for drugs, fighting, and stolen vehicle charges. This downward cycle continued from 1986 to 2000. Five kids and a marriage later, things just kept spinning out of control. During this time, I lost my second son at birth, broke up with my kids' mother. Then I met Valeska, got married and just a few years later we were in the midst of a divorce, I was still strung on drugs and alcohol, fighting for my sanity.

On May 22, 2000, my life took a turn I had never seen coming. I walked into the house of God and received the mercy and grace of His son Jesus Christ in my life. From that time 2000 until now 2024 as I draft this book, God has done some amazing things in my life. In 2000 God delivered from cocaine and alcohol. Twenty-four years of drinking and 20 years of doing cocaine and here I was clean and alcohol free.

In 2004, God delivered me from smoking marijuana and from cigarettes and took away the desire to need both. Also, that year I was ordained as a Deacon of Gospel Tabernacle Outreach Ministries. That year I reached out to my mother to let her know I forgave her. God was doing amazing things in my life and things were changing in me.

In 2008 I went back to school and received my GED and even scored a perfect eight hundred on the reading and writing part of the test. Let me tell you, English was my toughest subject in school because of my speech impediment and my difficulty in learning and obtaining information. So, to score a perfect eight hundred on that test is truly nobody but GOD! I have gone on to help pass a bill in the Rhode Island State House called "Ban The Box" bill and stood before senators and congressmen, I have held many titles in job positions that I was not qualified for in the eyes of men and have ministered to many in the same prison systems I was locked up in. God has taken me to places in my life that were impossible for me to achieve on my own and has done things in me and through me that I know without a doubt it was by Him and Him alone.

God said He would take the foolish to confound the wise and take the weak to confound the mighty. I was and still am at times the weak and foolish one He uses. God will take a mess and make it a message. Those whom society has looked down on and called throw-a-ways God will take and use for His glory. Now I live my life down here in Florida as an Operations Manager of a large community in Saint John's Florida serving God and enjoying life to its fullest. A high school dropout with no future ahead of himself living the blessed life in Christ because of one decision and one decision only and that was letting Jesus into my heart and allowing Him to be Lord over my life. Now don't get me wrong, life isn't perfect, and neither am I. But I serve a God who is, and He shows Himself faithful to me every day even at times when I don't deserve it.

Scripture says that "God is no respecter of persons." **Romans 2:11**. The same God who has done it for me wants too also do it for you. He makes broken things beautiful and wants to take the shattered pieces of your life and make a beautiful artwork for His glory out of it. God can and will do it. You just have to open your heart to Him and let His son Jesus in. Today make that choice and watch life change for the better. With God, you cannot and will not fail. Will God, do it? Yes, He can, let Him do it in you today. By Faith believe and you shall receive.

10. ONE SWEET SEASON TAUGHT ME SO MUCH

~In Loving Memory to Bishop Clarence E Lassiter~

"To Every Thing, There Is A Season, And Time To Every Purpose Under The Heaven." -Ecclesiastes 3:1

I have been through many different seasons in my Christian Walk. Some I cherish and some I look back on and realize that it was nobody but God. There is one season I wished lasted longer because in the 4 years I was in it, I learned so much. I have had a lot of people come in and out of my life over the years and have learned some are made for a lifetime and others for a twinkling of an eye. Out of all of these people, there is one that God blessed me to have met who made a significant impact on my life in the brief time he was in it. This gentleman's name is Bishop Clarence E. Lassiter.

Bishop was the co-founder of Gospel Tabernacle Outreach Ministries Inc., along with his beautiful wife and my spiritual mom in Christ Rev. Marilyn Lassiter. Bishop Lassiter was a man of few words but when he spoke it was with the authority of God and was always a teaching moment. Shortly after stepping into GTOM, bishop took me under his wing. I remember the day like it was yesterday. I was in my basement getting high and a white caddy pulled up in front of my house. Bishop was sitting in the car telling me to take a ride with him. I was only in the church for a couple of weeks and was smelling like drugs and alcohol and I was trying to make every excuse known to mankind why I could not go but Bishop was not taking any of my excuses that day. I got in his car, and I could tell he smelled weed and alcohol on me, yet he never said a word. He asked if I was hungry, to which I answered no, and he began to drive off. After about a ten-minute drive we ended up in front of the church and he asked me to come in. He proceeded to the bottom half of the Church to the back where there was a room filled with an old pool table and a few other items. He showed me this room and told me he wanted to make it a Prayer Room and that I was supposed to be the one to paint it. Now I was high as all heck and began to wonder if Bishop caught a contact from me being in the car. I asked Him to please repeat what he just said, and he told me You are to clean out this room, paint it, and get it ready to be our new prayer room. I explained to him that I wasn't that guy, thanks but no thanks and then he looked at me and said, "you are just who God needs to do it" and walked off.

I stood there looking into this room wondering to myself what was going on. Bishop came back with paint supplies and tools and asked how much do you want an hour? I still did not understand what was going on or how I ended up here, but I knew saying no was not going to be an option. So, I said $10 an hour hoping it would be too high a price, but the bishop looked at me and said in his deep voice "Praise God, when can you get started?" I went back the next day and that is when it began. What others had seen in me was someone not worthy of the time of day, unless I had something they wanted but that day, this man saw ministry. He began to pour into my life lessons and things that I continue to carry to this day. Every day Bishop would pick me up and bring me to the church where he sat to talk and began ministering to me about issues I was going through.

One lesson he taught me was about pedestals which I still teach today. I was on the ladder painting at the time, and He was telling me his life story about how he had been through many of the addictions and issues I faced and how God changed his life around. I looked down from the ladder and said, "wow I truly admire you, sir," he looked at me with a

39

little stern look and said "no, never do that." It caught me off guard because I didn't know what I had done. Then he began to teach. He looked and said "Son, see how you are on the ladder, and I am down here preventing you from falling? I answered "yes" and then he said, "when I am down here holding you up, if you fall, I can catch you and keep you from serious injury." Then he said, "but if you and I are both standing on the ladder together and we fall, we both get hurt and there is no one to catch us." "See, son never place anyone on a pedestal where you admire or look up to them because when they fall, you fall with them because you make them out to be bigger than what they are. Remember we're all flawed, and all come with something we deal with, and we should be holding each other up in prayer so when one falls the other can catch him. We are equals in the eyes of God and I am a man just like you who needs a savior just as much as you do." I understood what he said at that moment and have taken that life lesson with me everywhere I go. I never look at someone to be better than me or less than me because of the words Bishop spoke on that day. See, that day he showed me that I was someone in God's eyes even though I thought I was the least of them. Every day after this he poured into my life and treated me with the love of God I had never seen from others.

I spent 3yrs of my life hanging out with Bishop and learning the ways of the church and learning the vision he had for it. Within less than a couple of months, I had keys to the building and began opening for Sunday services and doing little things around the church to help out. I was learning so much and felt like this was the person I needed in life to help me find the man I was supposed to be. But then I received some tragic news that bishop had been diagnosed with cancer and my world came to a halt. I will never forget that meeting my wife and I had with him and his wife Rev. Marilyn, when he told us what was going on. He looked across the table in the conference room and said, "my son" you are the next Gospel Tabernacle, and I need you to keep going." I laughed like yeah ok, sure I am. Then Rev. Marilyn gave us the news. It felt like a gut punch from Mike Tyson. The car ride home from church was quiet as I didn't know how to process this. A couple of months past and the cancer had spread, and Bishop went home to be with the Lord.

That season of my life with him had ended and my mentor was no longer around. I was hurt and angry for a while. I didn't understand how God could finally put a man in my life worth following and someone who genuinely cared about me and then take him from me so quickly. I understand now that he was there for the season. I needed him and vice versa. I was used to complete some of the visions that God had given bishop for the church, like the prayer room and bookstore being formed and areas in the church being painted before he passed. We met each other at the God appointed time and God placed him in my life to help me grow in that brief time I knew him.

The day Bishop passed was a very tough time, but his lessons stayed with me. If there was ever a time that the scripture Iron Sharpens Iron were ever truly lived out, it was through the life and ministry of Clarence E. Lassiter. I have had many great men of God in my life, and I am grateful for them all but Bishop, well he was my spiritual dad and my friend. He is one of the reasons I can write this book today, because of the love he showed me, the lessons he taught me, and the life he lived that spoke more than words. For a short season, God allowed him to come into my life and make an impact that has also impacted others and for that, I am truly thankful for even the short amount of time I spent with him.

One of the things Bishop would say to me often (because I was a know-it-all) was "Always Remain Teachable." This lesson I still stand on today. God can send someone into your life for the briefest of moments and can teach you things you would never imagine, so you must remain open to receiving what they have to teach. After the Bishop passed, God filled the void of godly men in my life with Pastor Pelham, Evangelist Ronnie, Evangelist Russell, Minister Andrew, Elder Lee, Deacon Lenny, and so many others. I am beyond blessed to have them in my corner.

Every once in a while, Bishop pops into my heart and I am thankful to God for him, because every man I mentioned after his passing, they all carry a little part of Bishop and something they learned from him and we all came together under one banner to serve in the house that God built and Bishop founded. The men of GTOM all represented in their own ways the vision God gave Bishop and many of us still carry that vision today. It was one short season I shared with Bishop, but so many lives changed because of his love and faithfulness to God. One man can make a difference, and I hope that as Bishop was to me, I can be that to another. Even if it is just for a short season.

In the words of Bishop Clarence E Lassiter:
"PRAISE GOD"

I am a better man for the season I had with you....

Chapter 11: I Am Where God Wants Me

Even There Shall Thy Hand Lead Me, And Thy Right Hand Shall Hold Me.
-Psalm 139:10

Earlier in the book I told you how I stood before Senators and Congressmen to help get a bill past called "Ban the Box" in Rhode Island. Well let me tell you what God did in that whole situation. In 2013, I was approached by a group who asked me if I would tell my story before some legislators and businessmen to help bring awareness to how people with convictions have a tough time finding employment. I turned them down a couple times and God kept dealing with me about having a testimony and not sharing it for His glory. So, a few weeks later I said yes, I would testify.

Shortly after they decided to make a video on my life and the lives of others who have been incarcerated and where they were now. I did the video and gave my testimony on what God did in my life and how he has kept and forgiven me even though the state still seen me as an ex-con. After the video was released, I was given an invite to come to the RI Statehouse to speak on the subject. I agreed and went to the hearing. I was not ready for what I walked into. I get there and there are cameras everywhere, reporters, legislators all around and a room full of people. I went in and sat down and listened to all the people get up and speak around me and everyone had some sort of big title and name recognition. Yet here I am, this ex-con, ex-drug dealer and addict and ex-alcoholic sitting around all these prestigious people wondering what am I doing here?

Finally, they call me, and I get up to speak; cameras are flashing, eyes are on me, and the room is silent. I go to speak and begin to stutter up a storm but then I mentioned the name of Jesus, and something happened. I was up there giving a sermon and speaking of the goodness of God and how he kept me even when I struggled after being released from jail. Now this whole time I am saying to myself in my mind, "What are you doing, and you don't belong here." Yet when I was finished speaking, people were clapping even though. I did not know what I said or how I did it. But now I know the spirit of God took over and He has His way in that room.

Afterwards, I was standing out in the lobby with a few reporters answering questions and this tall gentleman with a cane walked up on me. He had salt and pepper hair and beard and reminded me a little of Colonel Sanders from KFC. He walks up and says "Mr. Parker, great speech in there." Then proceeds to say, "you want to know the difference between me and you?" I said, "yes sir please tell me." He looks me dead in the eye and says, "I am a congressmen and you sir are an ex-con." Now I began to get ready to rip this man in the hallway in front of all the cameras, reporters, and others but a still voice on the inside of me said "be still and hold your peace." So, I smiled and said, 'yes sir I am." Then something happened that let me know I was supposed to be there. The congressmen looked at me and said, "Do you want to know the difference between the two? You got caught and I didn't." My mouth dropped and I just stood there.

At that moment God showed me I was where I was supposed to be. I kept questioning why I was there and for what was my role in this? God showed me at that moment He had me there for such a time as this. I learned that day that God is in full control even when I am unsure of what, where, when, why and how. See God will never lead you someplace that will bring embarrassment to His name. Every place He leads you works for His glory as long as you follow His direction. That day he said, "just go open your mouth and I will do the rest." Well, I did, and He did. Afterwards the congressmen and I spoke for a little while longer and he informed me that he was going to vote for the bill to pass.

A few weeks later the bill passed with a majority of votes and is still law today. This is what God does when you choose to follow His leading. He doesn't care about your background, your status, bank statements, flaws, failures, or upbringing. He just wants to know do you trust Him, and will you move when he says move? Since that day I have never been shy about doing what God has asked of me, no matter how big or how small. What I learned on that day and every day since, is that there is nothing too big for my God. Trust him today to lead you, know he will supply every need for you to accomplish all he has called for you to do. God will direct your path and then walk with you through it to completion.

CLOSING COMMENTS

"SURELY GOODNESS AND MERCY SHALL FOLLOW ME ALL THE DAYS OF MY LIFE: AND I WILL DWELL IN THE HOUSE OF THE LORD FOREVER."

-PSALM 23:6

As I look back over my life and all that I have been through, I now see God was with me through it all. The good the bad and the ugly, God's hand was seeing me through. I didn't understand why I faced all that I did, but I see how God is now using it to bring Him glory. He brought me from Misery to Ministry. All that I have faced in life, I now use to help others see that there is a way to make it over your faults, failings, and circumstances. That way is to allow Jesus Christ, the way maker into your heart and allow him to do with your life what you in yourself could never do. I look back at all the times I have been in and out of jail, the fights that ended in gunfire and the bullets that missed me, the amount of drugs and alcohol that I have consumed in life that should have taken me out, and the mess I was in due to the lifestyle I lived. I can stand here and say today that Goodness and Mercy have followed me because if it hadn't I would and should be dead and gone.

There are so many more stories I can share with you all about how God brought me through but if I tried to share them in this book, it would be too thick to read. But I hope and pray that what I have shared will help you understand that the life you have been dealt, doesn't mean it has to be the life that is played for eternity. What I mean is this, those same things the enemy meant to use for evil to destroy you, God wants to use for His good to elevate you into eternal life.

46

Twenty-four years ago, I said yes to Jesus Christ and who I am today is not who I once was. People who hear my testimonies don't believe me when I tell them the man I used to be and that is all because of God.

So, if you are reading this in your jail cell or right in the comforts of your own home, I need you to know this, God can direct your path and bring you from where you are to where he has for you to be. You must take that first step and place your hand in the hand of the man who parted the Red Sea and then let him lead you to the other side. I thank you all for taking this journey through my past with me and I hope this book helps just one person come to the knowledge and wisdom of God. He can make you someone new. How do I know this? If he can take a wretch like me and bring me from Misery to Ministry, then he can do it for you also. Open your heart to Him and let Jesus take the wheel. Then hold on to Him and don't let go. It can be a little bit of a bumpy ride, but the destination is worth it.

About the Author

In this book "Blessed, From Misery to Ministry," author Jay Parker discusses the difficulties and barriers he had to endure as a young man and even into adulthood. He shares in his writings that no matter how badly he was treated and abused by the very people who were supposed to nurture and protect him, God kept him. By accepting God's help, he was able to break free from the hurt and mentality that came with it. He authored this book in the hope of helping you do the same. This turn-around was not just for his benefit but also for those around him. Jay's life clearly demonstrates that.

While serving at God at Gospel Tabernacle Outreach Ministries Incorporated, he learned how to fight evil with God's word rather than with his hands. He learned that there really are kind-loving people willing to help a man, encourage a man and even help a man heal. His mentors were the extension of the God he absolutely needed in life and so do you. He went from selfish, self-serving thinking to a true servant of God and of the people. He doesn't just carry titles given; he lives' them out. I pray one day you will do the same.

-Valeska Parker

www.ingramcontent.com/pod-product-compliance
Lightning Source LLC
Chambersburg PA
CBHW060141150626
46550CB00015B/2576